MINIMALISM

THE JAPANESE ART OF DECLUTTER TO ORGANIZE YOUR HOME LIFE

KIKU KATANA

Be content with what you have;
rejoice in the way things are.
When you realize there is nothing lacking,
the whole world belongs to you.

— LAO TZU

MINIMALISM

THE JAPANESE ART OF DECLUTTER TO ORGANIZE YOUR HOME LIFE

KIKU KATANA

CONTENTS

INTRODUCTION

Minimalism is about reducing how much investment you place in things which are congesting your life. It is not just about minimizing the stuff you own. This inevitably happens once you start on the path of minimalism. It is about considering the things and experiences in which you are investing too much of your time and not giving you joy. Consider minimizing their effect on you or removing them entirely. In other words, minimalism can be said to be a form of tumor surgery on your life where the tumors are all the harmful, addictive, and time-consuming things within your life. It is also a lifestyle which is to say that minimalism has to be practiced on a daily basis and not just when you need to free up space. It also applies to various areas of your life. This book deals with minimalism in different facets of life from clothing, pets, and the home to storage options and specific tips. The book champions minimalism as a favorable lifestyle which can positively influence friends and family but not be imposed upon them. It should not put stress on significant relationships. You can exist as individuals following different paths but still, have the same strong bonds.

Much of this book may sound like it is more about frugality than minimalism. That's because these two concepts have so much overlap in their thinking that they are naturally and permanently intertwined with each other. The same thought processes permeate both ideas and cannot be entirely separated. Frugality is minimalism, as it pertains to finances, and minimalism is frugality, as it relates to things and space. Remember that as we go.

WHAT IS MINIMALISM?

In recent times, minimalism has become one of the main trends even though it refers to a concept which has been around for thousands of years. Now we see it in the mainstream media, and it is being used in different areas of fashion, food, technology, and housing. Traditionally, minimalism was connected to pure intentional art and design concepts in the Japanese culture, but it is far more than that. It is a lifestyle which allows people to reduce their tethering to the material. It is marked with purpose and intentionality. At the center, you might call it the promotion of things which are most valued and it removes everything which distracts the audience from it. It refers to a life which forces intentionality. In the end, it creates improvements in the different elements of a person's life.

Mainstream media has made society buy into the deception that the good life is seen in the accumulation of things and possessing as many things as possible. The belief is more is better, and society has subscribed to the idea that happiness is something which can be purchased by a credit card at a store. This could not be further from the truth. The fact is minimalism brings freedom. It allows people to get off the continual treadmill of consumerism so to speak and will enable one to seek happiness in other aspects. During this time, it allows for friendships to grow and experiences to become that much richer as caring is separated from what you can buy each other and it becomes more about the experiences that you have together.

The present world goes at a breakneck pace. People are too hurried and stressed. They also work for long hours of the day in order to meet their obligations though they still end up falling into debt situations. They also rush from one activity to the next and even multitask though they still do not manage to be at rest when everything is done. They remain constantly connected with others via their cell phones although the life-changing relationships elude them. Minimalism allows for life to slow down so that you can be unencumbered and it frees you from the fever to live at a faster pace. It permits you to keep only what you need so that you only exist on what is significant.

Even though no one intentionally chooses to do so, many people are caught up in duplicity. They live one life bound to their family, another for their colleagues and another for the neighbors or social circles. The lifestyle they choose forces them to illustrate a particular external image which depends on their circumstance. They are frazzled by the recent projects or demands from their employer. The simple, minimalist life, on the other hand, is consistent and united. It practices a lifestyle which is flexible regardless of the scenario.

Minimalism Is Counter-Cultural

Current society not only idolizes material things regarding food and objects, but it also places incredible value on fame and celebrities. They are photographed and regularly interviewed to provide content for entertainment which is then fed to the masses at a fee. Their lives as seen on screen are held as the gold standard by which everyone should aspire. Those who live minimalist lives are not similarly championed through the media. They do not fit into the consumerist culture which is promoted by the corporations that sell products or by politicians who sell ideas. While most chase after success and their version of fame, minimalism goes against all of this and invites the individual to take a breath and consume less and instead focus on the experiences to be had. Similarly, when you come across a person living a life which has been simplified, you would probably recognize that you have been looking for the wrong things the entire time.

The process of minimalism is both empowering and challenging to people. Just saying "no" is hard to do but it will empower you as the individual to live life the way you want. So that you know what minimalism is and the benefits of it, here are some actionable steps to get you on the path.

1. List the current commitments that you may have.
2. Set priorities for those responsibilities from most to least essential.
3. Eliminate the least essential ones in sequence.
4. Start the process every month up to the point you are only doing things which give the most value.
5. Say no to the things which do not move you in the direction that you would like to go.
6. Sincerely ask yourself if you honestly need something.

Misconceptions

There is no right answer to this question of what minimalism is. The concept is open to analysis. As opposed to trying to include everything in minimalism, it would be better to try and ascertain what it is not. There are several misconceptions concerning minimalism. By addressing them, you can start to understand that it is not attainable for everyone.

Minimalism Is About Getting Rid of All Things You Possess.

It is true that a large part of minimalism is the removal of things from your life. However, the focus on minimalism should not be concerning what you are ridding from your life. The concentration should be on what is gained when you let go of the excess things that do not deliver value in your life. As opposed to focusing on what you need to get rid of, instead look at what minimalism brings to the table. Minimalism provides more space, time, peace and freedom. It is not about deprivation here.

It is about intentionally choosing to live with fewer things so that you may have more space and time for the essential things in your life.

Minimalism and Being Frugal Are One and the Same

Being frugal is about looking for opportunities where you can save on resources. The minimalist lifestyle may lead one to spend in a more careful manner and save funds as one buys less and shops in a more intentional way. Being frugal though is not the primary intention when it comes to being a minimalist. There happens to be an overlap between being frugal and being a minimalist because they both promote the concept of being intentional concerning the way that one spends their money. There are some who turn towards minimalism to be more frugal. Although, minimalism and frugality are not the same things.

Minimalism is more than just having less to saving money. It is about living with less money so that you have the time and space for the things that matter in your life. At the same time, minimalists make a choice to purchase fewer things although they buy items which are of high quality. They are still intentional concerning their spending by purchasing fewer things. They may not be focused on practicality as they are not willing to pay more even if it is a high-quality item. They would prefer to minimize spending on assets entirely because saving money is the end goal.

You Cannot Have Collections If You Are a Minimalist.

One of the misconceptions is that you are not allowed to keep things you like, or that you may not keep collections of things that give you happiness. Minimalism does not endorse getting rid of everything that you possess. It just means that you have to be intentional about the things that you do keep. That would mean curating possessions to the only items that you love and can use. Getting rid of the excess stuff means you can utilize and enjoy the things which you love even more. The critical thing when it comes to minimalism is moderation. As opposed to having 14 collections, you can opt to have just one or two of the items which you like the most. It may also mean that you trim the collection to the best pieces so that you are able to highlight these pieces and not lose sight of them as you might in an overgrown collection.

If you have a hobby which requires storing physical supplies, it is possible to designate a space in which you would keep the supplies and then be intentional and limiting the things that you store in this particular space. It is also about intentionally curating the things that are saved. Keeping only the supplies which would be actually used rather than just stockpiling all those supplies which are seldom used. Minimalism does not mean that you deprive yourself of things that you like or activities that you enjoy doing, but it should only be done in a way that would be significant and not just for the sake of itself. The entire point when it comes to minimalism is the removal of the excesses so you can concentrate on the things that you value and utilize the things that you enjoy and love.

Minimalism Is Equated to Stark All White Rooms Which Are Devoid of Life.

When people talk about minimalism, the first thing that comes to mind is all white dull and dreary rooms which do not have any décor or furniture. This is not the only way to achieve minimalism. It does not have to look a certain way.

A room following the minimalist orientation may also be colorful with candles, throw blankets and pillows. It is a success when the only things that you keep in your space happen to be the ones that you use and love the most. It needs to be personal and unique for your pleasure, so every person's version is going to be different from this perspective. It is about finding the right amount of things for your use. Determining what is enough may be different for everyone. The main thing is to only keep what would add value to your life and then dispense with everything else. So long as everything within your living area is something that you use a lot or you love then that is minimalism. You need to be specific concerning what you want minimalism to be within your living area. For one, the phrase cozy minimalism is descriptive of a space which is not cluttered and minimal though it is still cozy. It can help to use terms like this to be particular and clear about your vision for minimalism. You can then use this vision for the creation of a minimalist home which would work for you. You don't need to be concerned with following the minimalist décor preferences of another individual.

You Need to Follow Certain Rules or Standards to Be a Minimalist.

There are people that are experimental with following rules such as living with less than a 100 items or having less than 37 pieces in their wardrobe. This is interestingly not the only way that a person can be a minimalist. The best thing about minimalism is someone may create their own set of rules. Those rules can evolve as a person's life continues to change. Experimenting with a set of rules may be exciting and challenging as an experience. However, you should not let yourself be turned off or feel confined because of these guidelines. You only need to figure what works for you. You should come to the realization that minimalism involves identifying that which you value the most and then removing everything that does not align with these values.

You Cannot Be a Minimalist If You Have Children. Minimalism Works Only for the Young and Single.

Anyone can decide to go on the path for minimalism. Where you live or your occupation or if you have a family are not relevant. In fact, the larger the family, the more benefits you would gain from minimalism. The more people that are in one's house, the more things that a person will have. Removal of excess and the adoption of a minimal lifestyle may be more significant within these families. A minimalist type of family may also be different as compared to a single minimalist. Neither is more or less minimalist as compared to the other. In each scenario, minimalism entails the identification of what you value the most and then removing of the excess so as to make more room for that which is cherished. Their values may differ so what they may keep and discard is also going to be different. Minimalism will work for any individual that is willing to put in the time and effort to remove the excess in their lives and make room for the things that matter most.

Minimalism Only Applies to Your Things.

Getting rid of the excess is one of the prominent aspects when it comes to minimalism. Although the physical materials are just one part of what is minimalism, it actually goes beyond what you have in your possession. It ought to be applied to everything in your life. It needs to be about deciding what adds value in your life and then removing the rest.

When you start living with this ideology, you may realize the minimalist lifestyle is more than just de-cluttering of your house. It may be applied to the way that you spend your time, the kind of consumer that you become and your financial situation.

Japanese art

A lot of the time, minimalism is linked with the traditional Zen style design. The Zen style arts and design usually focus on the elimination of frills that are not necessary. These arts are typically described as aesthetics related to subtraction because they enable great beauty to emerge from less as opposed to more. A lot of creative power has been poured into the identification and removal of what is unnecessary irrespective of the dimension, shape, space or color. When it comes to Zen-style arts, single line or single elements may tend to exhibit potential without bounds. If you would like to introduce Zen style minimalist designs, there are several things to consider which are usually like traditional Japanese aesthetics. The critical thing is ultimately the aesthetics and also about being conscious of the person's relationship with nature. This consciousness reveals itself through the behaviors of individuals. One may remember that traditional Japanese minimalist design would be the one that then inspires you so that you concentrate on behavior and the environment. It is much more than the minimalist appearance. The influenced design is commonly admired for its simplicity and minimalist mode. People find that the essence of less is more in the quiet Zen approaches.

Though Zen art is a variation of the entire Japanese traditional culture stretching thousands of years, it is as if Zen ended up with the representation of what the world would see is Japanese aesthetics. The question is how it happened and why Zen-influenced arts and design embrace simplicity.

Japanese Traditional Design

It is possible to trace the origin of Japanese design to the 6th and 7th centuries through architecture like Ise-Jingu or Horyuji. Zen arts and design are quite newer though as Zen was actually brought to Japan from China during the 12th century and the Zen-inspired culture like Zen garden, ikebana, tea ceremony or Nou Theater cemented the foundation during the time of the middle ages. It is crucial to remember the emergence of Zen arts corresponded with the renaissance. Although the Renaissance design was robust and symmetrically balanced, perspective and proportions for the depiction of the real face of nature and humans for Zen arts, focused entirely on different elements; subdued pleasure and subtractions of ambiguities and elemental decay as opposed to vibrancy and asymmetries. Although, of course, Zen is just one perspective when it comes to Japanese society.

A number of arts and culture did not embrace simple and minimal as opposed to other popular decors. In any case, the Japanese attitude which fascinated western societies was not about the décor element of the design but the simplistic nature. The European artists were also amazed at the time they came to discover Ukiyo in the late 19th century when architects found an alternate form of modernism in Katsura Rikyu during the early 20th century. Overall, simple aesthetics concerning Japanese culture has influenced modern art and design in a significant manner. One has to consider that Zen arts are just one particular form of Japanese traditional culture. For example, Ukiyo-e was well known as pop art for the Edo era, and not Zen art. Katsura Rikyu was constructed by an imperial family which was in Kyoto and did not reference a Zen temple. The influence of

Zen aesthetics is a bit obvious. They consider simplified but bold perspectives and compositions, reduced number of elements and they claim to be effective for the elevation of natural beauty into artistic forms of simplification.

It may be said that Zen arts, despite their limited presence in the modern era, held an underlying belief that the Japanese were nurturing it for thousands of years and then crystallized it in a universal manner. A number of the design modes do not happen to be explicitly Zen though they still embody the spirit of Zen as an aesthetic. The essence captivated in such a manner that it would inspire people around the world.

Japan's New Minimalists

Japan has become one of the main hotbeds for minimalism. The country is very familiar with ascetic philosophies in the form of traditional Zen Buddhism, and so minimalism seems like a good fit. A number of young adherents though are taking it to the next level by emptying their lives of materials things. They are now removing possessions from their already small apartments to a point which seems inhumane when it comes to typical western standards. An example who was used in several articles two years ago was Take Fumio

Sasaki, a 38-year-old book editor who lives in a single room apartment in the Japanese capital city, Tokyo.

He has four pairs of pants, four pairs of socks and three shirts. There is not much else that the editor owns. The transformation he underwent on this path apparently took place two years ago when he became tired of attempting to keep up with the trends or maintaining a collection of books, CDs and DVDs. He decided then to chuck everything and allegedly it was not as hard as one would think. He later wrote a book about his new approach to life titled 'We Don't Need Things Anymore.' In the book, he gave an explanation concerning his version of minimalism which was initially utilized in the field of politics and the arts that believed in the idea of reducing things to the bare minimum.

Currently, Sasaki says that he owns 300 items. He implies that he used to hold 10 times of what he does at present and that he was not happy with that kind of existence at the time. Sasaki would find himself at the point where he was always assessing his self-worth on the things that he owned or did not own. This would be used as some sort of measuring stick, and he never liked how he measured up.

Sasaki came to the realization concerning danshari which is also a Japanese concept for de-cluttering and started on books by Marie Kondo who had an idea related to keeping things that create joy which was so ubiquitous that it actually got name-dropped in the reboot of Gilmore Girls. It took him about 6 years before he was able to fully de-clutter his life which was apparently 'maximalist.'

For him and many of the young Japanese population, it is not about how little that one has but the way it makes one feel. Sasaki gives his minimalist lifestyle credit for helping him with loss of excess weight and becoming proactive and extroverted. He states that minimalism is just one of the many entries there is to a happier existence. If individuals have a lot of things in their home, but they still able to maintain relationships and feel satisfied, he then thinks that the mission has been accomplished.

Another hardcore minimalist is a 30-year old that opted to discard his bed because it was tiresome for cleaning and now he wears only ten outfits during an entire year, reads digital books and cooks using one pot. Another by the name Elisa Sasaki spent a month living from one bag and returned home in order to reduce her closet to 20 items of clothing and 6 pairs of shoes. At present, it would seem that her room is a vast open space. The other is Katsuya Toyoda who is an online editor that only has one table and a futon on his apartment which is 230 square feet.

There are even some Japanese families with young children who are also embracing the theme of minimalism which is a big contrast from the western-style parenting that is steeped in materialism. A homemaker from Kanagawa Prefecture claimed that she switched decorating her home for clearing it out and her husband and children followed in her stead. At present, her daughter only wears two pairs of jeans on different days.

There was a photo collection of minimalist Japanese homes which illustrated Naoki Numahata, a freelance writer pushing his daughter's chair to a table in a room which was empty except for some curtains on the window. There were only a few clothes hanging in the closet in another photo.

Though the thought of having a home which is empty instills terror into some people, there is a certain appeal of not being distracted by the clutter of things. Similarly, it would also allow for one to entertain or educate in other areas like through outdoor playing and traveling.

The idea is quite appealing though for the urban dwellers. When one thinks about their home located in a small rural setting, you might find that many of your possessions are related to the quest for self-sufficiency and specialized appliances for making things from scratch, gardening tools and boxes of clothing for different seasons. There is a sense of independence which you have when you own your tools or materials for the task because it is not possible to rely on a support community to get these. The Japanese minimalists claim their lifestyle may save them in different ways when it comes to environmental events. For example, in 2011, the Tsunami initiated by an earthquake killed more than 20,000 people and caused injuries to many more. Apparently, 30 to 50 percent of the injuries that came from earthquakes have been caused by falling objects which oddly serves as an incentive for minimalism. It is now easy to understand minimalism in this aspect in Japan and why it can be taken to extreme levels. When you have a lot of stuff, it suddenly becomes a threat when you are in an earthquake-prone area because they all become potential projectiles. It is better to have less to worry about in the event of a disaster.

Why Minimalism

Simplistic lifestyles and mindsets related to living with as little as possible have been around for centuries, and it has not always been the Amish and the monks taking on a Spartan lifestyle. The World War 2 economy brought a lot of consumerism and the American Dream which is geared towards getting a good job or having a house, car, and family. This arrived with the 'Keeping Up with the Joneses' mentality which has been there up to the present. For example, during the 60s hippies and the communes sought to break from this material living. Before them, the Greek Epicureans tried to break the cycle so to speak. Although strides have been made, it would be fair to conclude that everyone's lives can use a bit of lightening up. Unfortunately, people just work themselves into the ground the entire week so they can buy more and more things. What is interesting is that no one actually believes that happiness is tied to the things that they own, but almost everyone lives as if there is a direct correlation. Personal levels of debt have also increased in a dramatic manner. So the problem is geared toward the relation between self-discipline, will and objective perspectives.

With that said, minimalism is not about getting rid of consumerism and clutter from a person's life. It's about finding your sense of self and then focusing on those things that you enjoy. It is also about the creation of a lifestyle which has been streamlined and focused on those individuals and ideas that enrich. It is the center of what makes you happy, and chances are it is not that boring office job.

Many people are beginning to consider minimalism as a

life choice, and recently there have been collective movements for living a simpler existence. Even top business executives are trading in penthouses for trailers.

Unchecked Consumerism

The current thinking teaches us that having possessions is how you define yourself in society. The consumerist type of mode for life dictates the things that you buy, how much you want to purchase, and the frequency of purchases. In this regard, they add advertisement through every entertainment portal, be it newsprint, television, radio, social media and other online platforms. These messages on what you should aspire to have been forced down our throats since the 20th century upon formation of the "American dream" concept. Society told its citizens henceforth that the only way to be a good person was to produce and to consume endlessly to the point of death and pass this knowledge on to the younger generations so that they could uphold the same tenets for their offspring as well.

The school system also taught children that the only way that a person would be productive in the society is in the event they work for things in a company that underpays them in order to buy things they might not use. This dangerous mindset pervades modern society not only in the western world but various areas of the globe because capitalism has become the predominant ideology. This mentality has also lead to the overconsumption of goods and resources which would place the planet under more burden and allow for economic systems to take advantage of the workers. Not only does the earth then suffer but the spirit of the citizen is also beaten down. It does not matter how hard that one tries to accumulate wealth; material possessions would never satisfy in a spiritual way. Through leading a lifestyle which is minimalist, you are able to shift your values then and align them in a way that creates a more environmentally fulfilling and socially just world.

The question is what happens when you get rid of all this stuff that you have accumulated. The results are beyond having a neater kitchen so to speak. You get room to focus on the more important things. You also gain breathing space so you can live in an intentional manner and then remove all the things that distract you from that which you value the most. You will also have clarity of mind to ask about the things that are most significant to you.

China Adds to the Problem

Since the advent of the technological boom in the east from both China and Japan, the western world has become flooded with their electronic products from televisions, radios, home theaters, mobile devices, and hundreds of thousands other little widgets. Unfortunately, these products have added to our vanity and keep us clinging to physical products. They have only perceived value, and not necessarily real value. Take, for example, smartphone giant Samsung has issued a version of the Galaxy Note every year for the previous decade. Every year, it would mean clients are scrambling for the next offering to keep up with the trend and buy the subsequent upgrades issued by Samsung for new devices. What happens is the device is provided at a high market price and then devalues when the next best thing gets out because it supposedly becomes obsolete.

The iPhone 5 cost an estimated eight hundred dollars at its debut in the market when it was launched, and it currently retails for $100 on E-bay and Amazon. Emotionally, the product still feels like it is valuable in this scenario especially since the price point for the gadget is irresistibly low for the consumer.

That is a high-end example, but what about low-end items. For instance, in the 1900's something as simple as a skillet had real value. It was made tough and lasted for generations, and maybe it was even handed down from your grandparents. It was something you kept because it was valuable, durable and long-lasting. In our brains, we still have that lingering memory of value that we associate with the skillet; that perceived value. In our minds, a skillet is not something you throw away.

In contrast, if you buy a skillet today, it may last six months, or even a year before the non-stick surface is no longer effective, or the handle comes loose. The best thing to do is throw it in the trash. But we can't. Emotionally, it still feels like something of value, and that prevents us from ditching it. Even though millions of skillets are being shipped out of China yearly at high volume, and low cost. We cannot throw this one away. This emotional attachment and perceived value are what keeps us collecting and hoarding items until our house is full of things.

When you consider the big picture, it is even worse though. The plastics from electronics have always been tricky to manage, especially since there is minimal domestic demand for the material. Sorting and contamination issues and long-standing environmental concerns on flame retardants have forced processors to start relying on the market for exports. The value of e-plastic took a significant hit in 2017. The CEO of New York company, Sunnking, Duane Beckett stated mixed e-plastic is basically useless considering the recent restrictions. Jim

Fei, the president of the brokerage firm Baycrest International, noted as well the price of e-plastics had dropped significantly since the ban on imports. Though this has hampered the movability of a low-value material, it has not entirely stopped it though. One way that Fei and others claimed this is occurring is via the Chinese firms going in another direction in Asia in order to keep the flows of North American e-plastic alive. The actions of the country are probably going to have a lasting effect on the global recycling market. Wong from the CSPA claimed that China had been preparing to ban the imports of every plastic scrap by the end of the current year though he noted particular forms of plastic scrap like washed flakes may be allowed for importation in 2018. A number of firms were even beginning to consider the long-term effects of this initiative.

———

 You have succeeded in life when all you really want is only what you really need.

—*Vernon Howard*

2

CHANGING YOUR THINKING

The minimalist mindset is a combination of thoughts, feelings, and desires. When you practice this manner of thought, then you focus on living with fewer things or doing less to eliminate that which is unnecessary. People should focus on experiences as opposed to the accumulation of wealth and physical objects. This system of thought means you must let go of those things which you are not using or do not really want and avoid bringing new things until and unless they satisfy a particular requirement. You have to think about it as a constant practice or sharpening of your mental and emotional skill set. Without the cultivation of a minimalist mindset, minimalism is an ongoing battle. You may try and resist temptations to reduce the physical and mental clutter and try to find natural solutions. However, the whole time, your urges may steadily build.

In the same way as extreme weight loss diets, minimalism without the mindset leaves one destined to relapse, and possibly in a big way. Pushing against a person's desires can be considered a losing battle. In this case, if battling against one's desires are not what minimalism is about then you might ask the question, what is this all about? This book is not here to tell you that you need to give up on your aims for a simpler life. On the contrary, the objective is to be realistic and to go about minimalism the right way. It is not going to be easy, but it's possible for one to change their desires through practice and actual desire.

When you are cultivating a minimalist mindset instead of just going through the motions and getting rid of things, it is not a losing battle. The motives are driven by your thoughts, and actions fall into place. You learn to love the simple life and see the reasons behind actions which people take as minimalists. The minimalist mindset is best considered as a reduction according to priorities.

It should not be concerning throwing things out and wishing that you get it back again. It is about making adjustments to reduce the material in your life and at a pace which is preferable for you. Over the course of time, you may then highlight that which is important. Objects are the most commonly envisioned cut back, though the minimalist mindset would also apply in the area of relationships, your relationship with yourself and activities, as well as other aspects of your life. The reduction is based according to priorities, so you need to make room concerning that which matters.

You can learn the minimalist mindset on your own through practicing the concept of minimalism on a regular basis, and in a method that is not forced, taking note of the way that affects your life. Though the mindset is the one that desires less, you should learn to be happy with that which you already have. Try and appreciate how much you have in your life already and realize that the relative value of material possessions, complicated lifestyles, and negative relationships is zero. Minimalism is a freedom from the things that you own and freedom from the desire to get more things which you may not necessarily need. You own the objects instead of the other way around. So, when you purchase things, you might want to form a checklist before-hand that considers why you'd like to go to that place or own this or that. In so doing, you will eventually come to a place where you find that life is to be shared and enjoyed rather than controlled and possessed. The minimalist type of mindset is a freedom from the modern kind of mania. It involves disengaging with the unnecessary elements in life which only serve to clog the physical and mental spaces. You should learn to refrain from things that would counter this intentionality such as gossiping and small talk which only serves to increase the level of your vanity. Living a simpler life means that you are not caught up with the latest news and trends. Minimalists also tend to live in a cleaner world with a less amount of production, consumption and so there is less waste. This desire for brighter future drives the lifestyle changes from within and living with less contributes to that objective. Minimalism does not relate to dogma though. There is no religion or a particular way of thinking about it. It is an internally driven urge for making reductions and prioritizing what would be valuable to you. It is done differently by different people though. You may be living in the tundra or in New York City and still be practicing minimalism because it is subjective.

It is a practice that comes from feelings and philosophies which initiate within each person. As you go into the realm of reduction and the world of simple but strong values, you may come to find your internal motivations so that minimalism is not really a struggle. Far from it, the actions needed to make the reductions will soon become natural.

How to Detach from Items

One of the core essences for minimalism involves detachment. Once complete, you are free to craft your physical world. A way to do this would be to execute a series of small breakups, and each time release the hold that the item has over you. It depends on what things you are into. For example, if you are into shopping for clothes, start to cancel subscriptions to magazines that just encourage you to buy this or that and stop watching shows which glorify wearing a certain level of designer fashion. You need to eliminate your connections to platforms that lead you to buy into these addictions. As such, that also means unsubscribing from pages on social media which concern shopping or the latest trends. The hardest thing would be to distance yourself from people that are bad influences in this regard. The interesting thing is that they may be best friends to you or even relatives. In either case, you will have to create a form of temporary distance while you build discipline. In time you will start to consider the items as a means of clothing yourself rather than as a status symbol, sense of entitlement or ego booster. They are not there to prove anything or to make you feel better about yourself, but they are there to cover you from the elements.

When you are done with the clothing addiction, you can settle and become comfortable with your new way of life before embarking on the next addiction in your life. For example, it may be unhealthy addictions to fast or processed food. There is such a thing. If you find yourself binge eating on several occasions or ordering too much and then having to put a lot of it in the trash, then that is a problem for minimalism to solve. From there you can use the same method you did with clothing and avoid triggers for ordering and fill the space with fresh food you personally find tasty yet healthy.

Resist being lazy. Instead, find a compromise which is both delicious and healthy. It is not hard to find a combination which allows for nutrition and satisfaction. The bottom line, in this case, is that stuff is not important. Fun is the thing that you need to concentrate on and pursuing your passion is also as significant as our relationships with people. All excess things do is draw our attention to them and detract from the relationships which we should be fostering with other people.

One way of changing your thought process which would allow for detachment is to consider the downside of your items. For example, a car is too expensive to buy, own and insure. A phone can be associated with distraction while a television encourages sloth. Shoes are expensive, and they have to be stored, and you can only wear a pair at a time. The great thing is books do not serve any purpose when they are not being read; in fact, they sit and just take up space.

You need to consider what life would be if you did not own each item. Would life be noticeably different if that item was not there? The other question is: do you have the ability to fulfill the main purpose of that item in another manner. For example, if you were driving a used Toyota as opposed to a Lexus, consider if it would prevent one from getting to work. In the event that a phone had a cracked screen and you had to use a cheap replacement, would it prevent you from communicating with those who are in your life? After coming to the realization that the world is not going to end with that item then it is much easier to break the attachment. You may also need to make a mental break from it through acknowledging its insignificance. It may also be useful to make a symbolic break through a detachment ceremony.

Lowering Your Overhead

Any business owner knows that increasing one's overhead is bad overall and can result in stagnant growth. However, people rarely look at their expenditure in this manner. People attach too much meaning to things, and so they lose sight of who they are. People are emotional about their purchases as they irrationally believe the clothes and the mortgage will bring security and happiness or fill the hole in their being. In fact, these things are what are decreasing the benefits of a person's life. So, you need to treat yourself in the same way you would monitor an upcoming startup and reduce the overall expenditure which is cutting into your net margin. A number of books and posts have been written concerning the way to become more mindful and intentional with your life. There are some which focus on the spiritual side of things while others consider the organizational side. Minimalism to decrease you overhead requires you to be ruthless with your ingrained logic and analyze whether existing and consuming adds value to your life. If not, you need to consider why you are continuing to do it. The perspective of looking at your life in the same way as a balance sheet or income statement allows you to place things in your life in the credit and debit sides. That way you will be able to prioritize what costs you have and actually look at them as liabilities instead of attachments. When you are done with the fixed costs and really important variable expenses, you can get rid of everything else.

Symbolic Means of Breaking Attachment to Things

Find an image or draw a picture of the item. This item is going to represent the item and the attachment that you feel for it. The next step will feel a bit goofy but just do it anyway. Say aloud 'I am no longer attached to this item. In detachment, there is freedom. I release my hold on this item.' Tear that paper into shreds or cast it into the fire. In order to enhance the detachment, you would then perform the ceremony with friends and family. Gather around the living room. Take turns releasing the attachment through stating that you are no longer attached to the object. After breaking attachment with the object, you will find that you are at ease more with the things you still own. It will also be easier for you to de-clutter the living environment. The added bonus is you will move away from the materialistic mentality.

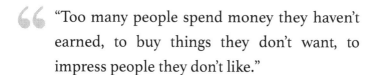 "Too many people spend money they haven't earned, to buy things they don't want, to impress people they don't like."

—*Will Rogers*

3

WHERE TO START

It may seem hard to believe but de-cluttering can be freeing. Knowing where to start though may be a big roadblock. If you have the desire to get some stuff out of the house then you may want to start with some of the following items that you would say goodbye to with little thought.

20 Things to Ditch Right Now Without Thinking

These are a few small and easy goals designed mostly to get you thinking in the right mindset of minimalism before you make any major and substantial changes.

1. Old magazines.

If you are keeping these so as to feel nostalgic or to look

back later on, you probably will not get around to it, especially if you have a busy schedule. You are not a doctor's office either. If you are keeping them for your children so they can make collages out of them later on then just keep three of them.

2. Expired coupons.

Many people like to put coupons away for a rainy day or in the event that you're going to redeem them. You can opt to put them in platforms such as Evernote with a delete tag and a deadline reminder so that you can eliminate the paper clutter altogether.

3. Trim your wallet.

Take out the cards in the wallet and go through which ones are usually needed. That means throwing away all of those cards which you know that you are never going to use, including the coffee loyalty cards, or business cards you got a few years ago. It also means any other cards which are rarely needed. The result, in this case, would be that you have less to carry and getting to the card that you actually need is going to be that much easier.

4. Unsubscribe to emails and newsletters.

If you live online, you are going to find yourself attached

to a number of online communities and subscriptions most of which were only for temporary research or task purposes. That way you find yourself swamped with endless subscriptions to different platforms from money markets to travel destinations. You become bombarded with so much noise on a daily basis that it even distracts you from important things. You only need to subscribe to things which would add value.

One subscription means loads of unsolicited emails so you need to be tough on this as your email address is going to be sold to others. Consider services such as 'Unroll Me' because they work well in order to clean one's inbox. You should also turn off the email notifications unless they are crucial. You need to get into the habit of deciding when you would like to see your emails as opposed to your emails governing the way your schedule works as that could bring excessive distraction.

5. Dispose of most of your credit cards.

This is one of the most painful moves to make because they are gateways for your addiction. You will find yourself making excuses as to why you need three cards at any one time when actually, you only need one. Similarly, when you go out, carry cash rather than the card to avoid overspending and only allow yourself the luxury of the card if you pay off your credit card debt every month. It is one less stress to have in your wallet and your mind because debt keeps you ineffective and complicates an otherwise simple life.

6. Changing your commute path.

Think about the path for commuting that you take in the morning. Ask yourself if you can improve the way that you travel. That does not mean that you have to take a faster route but it may mean that you take a nicer one or a more comfortable way of traveling. This does not mean you need to stress yourself, battling the clock to get to work. You need to make it that much more enjoyable and use it in a wise manner. So, take the time and meditate and then relax on your path to work. You may decide to replace the drive to work with a bicycle path or a train depending on what would relax you more. Mix up the commute to work as these minor changes can make a significant difference.

7. Take out the plastic bags.

You get plastic bags every time you buy something from a store in order to carry things. Though once you get home, the bags become obsolete and they start cluttering everything in the home. Considering that you will always have an influx of bags and carrier packages in the house especially if you tend to buy things online, you should stay ahead of the curve and consistently dispose of them because they will always be available.

8. Get rid of your smartphone.

Now, this sounds a bit extreme and impossible for most in this modern age, but there is a point to it. What is not usually admitted in today's social circles is that smartphones can be just as addictive as alcohol and other drugs. Everyone is a big fan but if you do not watch it, you might find yourself using it when you are not doing anything else. It becomes your go-to thing because it is what allegedly connects you to the outside world by filling you up with useless information, mentally exhausting you and keeping you distracted from that which really matters. If you are the type to quickly end a conversation so you can bury yourself in a phone or cannot deal with an awkward silence without referring to social media, then this might just be for you. Now obviously this does not mean that you should end all communication with everyone in your circle. Go back to the basics and get yourself a phone that allows for short message texting and calls alone, no social media. Try it for one month and see how it goes. Many things that you are using the smartphone for are what you might call time fillers. You can read emails at home or when you are at work.

9. Lesser or zero social media.

This is another big one that is going to be hard to leave especially if you work or operate in an environment that has electronic devices such as PCs and mobile devices. Social media is a big time-filler which can possess you for hours on end and there are several options to keep your attention honed on different subjects. This includes Facebook which is the typical source of what is going on in people's lives to Twitter which can be used for political rants and meme creation. Between these two and YouTube, one can end up spending their entire day online without getting anything done when it needs to be done. This is not to say that you need to completely ditch social media. You might want to reduce your log-on sessions on one or two platforms.

If you happen to be on Facebook, Twitter, Youtube, Snapchat, and Instagram, perhaps you could keep it to just two platforms like Facebook and Twitter. The next thing to do is reduce the time that you spend on social media. Set up a schedule of your time allotted to social media every day and reduce it in half. If your schedule shows that you spend an average of 6 hours every day on social media, or online for any purpose, reduce that time to three hours if possible. Before you know it, you will be able to go days without logging on social media and not notice it because you will have filled your days with other enriching experiences and tasks.

10. Slow down and breathe.

Life can be quite busy, especially if you have a family because between the children, spouse, and work, you may get overwhelmed mentally and emotionally. These are all factors that clog up your mind and which need to be sifted through so that you can enjoy a simpler existence. Take time to slow down and enjoy where you are as an individual and appreciate what you have or the problems that you are going through. Simply enjoy the moment regardless of where you may be. Get out of the office at work or out of the house and go for a stroll. Read something non-technical for 20 minutes in a quiet place. When things get to be too much, as they sometimes can, try and concentrate on your breathing. This will focus your mental strength and calm you down.

11. Eating less and healthier.

Dietary plans have been essential to simple life constructs for ages and for good reason. The right diet allows you to live your days better. For one, you will probably sleep better and have better energy levels during the day. There are several secrets behind what you eat, and the times you eat which control the energy levels and motivations we have to live life. As such eat a big breakfast, a small lunch, and a tiny dinner. If you are sitting at a desk then you are not burning a lot of energy and so there is no need to have three big meals. You can have a meaty breakfast, then snack on salads and nuts for lunch. Then you can do a snack for dinner of whatever happens to be in your fringe.

12. Drink less alcohol.

This is very straightforward. Reduce the days of drinking alcohol in a week that you usually do and when you do go drink out, or in your house, limit the intake. Drinking too much alcohol disorients and disorganizes your schedule which in turn makes you less productive. You do not sleep well when you drink too much which then messes up your to-do list when you wake up and the entire day because you will be exhausted and lack the motivation to do anything effectively considering the symptoms of a hangover.

It is also unappealing for your image at a particular age. Don't get me wrong. Drinking and partying is normal at particular ages when you are young and do not have as many obligations but when you are married and have children, it is not a good look. It is also a burden on your wallet as you are prone to making bad decisions under the influence of alcohol including buying things you do not need or going on expensive excursions on the spur of the moment because alcohol lowers the brains inhibitions which are the protective gates of the mind including the centers for safety and obligation. So, you can ruin a lot in your life due to drinking including your family and health. Reducing it or quitting altogether allows you to have better energy levels and places less of a strain on your finances.

13. Reduce the to-do list.

Whether it's taking a number of online courses, reading a few books or just trying to achieve too much at once can be quite taxing for anyone. In time, it can mentally and emotionally wear you down to the point of burnout. As such, you may want to focus on that which is significant and downgrade what is small or less important. Then do one big thing at a time. Only start a new one upon completing the last one. Then you should also be sure to say no to things that may make the list unmanageable.

14. Clear the desktop screen of your PC.

This especially applies if you are the type to work online or spend a lot of time on the computer. The PC represents a workstation and should be organized so that you are easily able to navigate your personal files and find things with ease. When everything is in disarray and the screen is filled with hundreds of shortcuts, you then it can be disorienting and is a representation of how clogged your psyche may be. Start using Google Drive or Dropbox if you need to keep the majority of them. At least the files will be stored in the cloud and you will be able to access them from anywhere on any PC. It is one less concern to worry about and the monthly fee to store them is manageable.

15. Less debt.

This is one of the big ones. Debt hampers emotional and mental functioning because of all the stress that it causes. If you owe a lot of people money, then there will be immense pressure to settle your bills because you will not be able to relax otherwise. Debts have the ability to remove your amenities and place you in a bad physical way because of the constant threat of debt collectors. The government also has the ability to incarcerate you in the event that you have debts with them. So, it is better for your mind and emotions if you start paying them off little by little rather than living with them or worse yet accumulating them. So, buy a simpler vehicle, using cash rather than a fancy one with a credit card thus increasing the size of your debt. You may decide to eliminate the items that have been causing a strain on finances and increasing debts such as the car, credit cards, and shopping. Make a budget and stick to it.

16. DVDs that you know you are never watching again.

There are those movies that you bought some years ago thinking they would be great but when you put them in the player, you did not survive the first fifteen minutes. You are never going to watch them again though you keep saying that you will set time for them and watch them through to the end. Now they take up space on the counter, table or wall unit and increase the amount of clutter. Stop wasting time on them and throw them out.

17. Shop less and buy online.

This sounds counter-intuitive especially since it entails the use of credit card purchases which can dig you into another hole but it does make sense. It limits the contact that you have going outside and being tempted to splurge. On the other hand, it makes it that much easier to have everything delivered on your doorstep. Support the local suppliers who can deliver online at a rate which is competitive. Finding small businesses that can do this can save you a lot of energy and time. You may automate the deliveries and payments thus reducing the things that you need to do.

18. Scan and Shred old paperwork.

This is something you can do early on as an easy win, so to speak. It would be advisable for you to get a hold of a scanner and a shredder. Scan any important documents and paperwork first. Once you have all the scans of your important documents saved in your online cloud storage (Google Drive or Dropbox), then shred everything and make sure that you recycle.

19. Clear your wardrobe.

This is also one of the easy wins that you can manage during the first few phases of your minimalism path. The first thing to do would be taking everything out of the wardrobe and piling it on the bed. The next thing would be to create 3 piles. These will consist of the things which are going to go to charity, to sell or to the trash. Anything that you have not worn during the previous 6 months ought to go to one of the piles. Then, you can work through each of the items and ask yourself the question of whether you truly need it. The rest of the items would go back into the wardrobe and they can be sectioned off into each wardrobe type of clothing. Less choice is indicative of less time spent thinking about what you need to wear.

20. Four-day work week.

This is the overall direction that people should be heading towards. In the event that you can supplement your 5th day of work from more earning and savings then it is indeed possible. The objective behind the four-day work week is to reduce the level of work-related stress caused by a full work week as is the case in many high functioning corporations. You hardly have time to focus on relationships, hobbies or other dreams you may have had while working on other income streams. The way our companies are set up is that they do not allow people to be diverse in their income streams or skill sets. Consider renting out car space with companies like Kerb. When you are on vacation, then you may opt to provide your home for rental purposes to earn more money or even rent out your car since you will not be using it. Think outside the box so as to change up the work week.

How to Get Your Family on Board

If you have already instilled minimalism into your life by adopting simple living, there are going to be a few issues when you introduce this mode of living to your loved ones. It is possible that those who are close will not be comfortable with this new direction in life. If your family jumps on board with your changes and participates in the journey towards a simpler life then that's great but for the vast majority, this is not the situation. For the ones who are going it alone, it can be helpful to prepare for push back and to know how to react in the best way when this occurs.

Start with Yourself

Before you help anyone with the journey you have to figure things out and start with your stuff and your spaces. This means being able to reap the benefits for yourself. Then you can proceed with the family and observe it as a process. It may take a bit of time but slowly and surely you will be able to win over the clutter-prone members of the house.

How to Win over Family Members That have yet to Adopt the Minimalist Lifestyle

Understand the Collector Mentality

If you have family members that are messy, they are probably born with the collecting gene. Collectors are the opposite of those who love to purge. The purgers feel that it is easy to clear space, and they get rid of that which is not needed so they tend to live within the moment. The collectors though have a lot of joy in the curation of items which give them nostalgia. Similarly, the collectors have the tendency of being inspired in scenarios where there is a lot of clutter as opposed to being stressed out by it. Because you are a minimalist, your mindset will probably be oriented in such a way that clutter makes you stressed. Among creatives, there are some who are collectors and so they are inspired by a bit of chaos around them. The others are purgers who are inspired by a clutter-free environment.

Listen

In order to win over the collectors that live with you, you need to show understanding for their habits, mindsets, and concerns. Then calm any fears concerning significant things being discarded. Make certain that they feel they can trust you because you know how they feel and they know that you will not get rid of things on impulse alone. Listen first to their side of the story and then you can bring up the topic of minimalism at a later time. Make certain that you understand all of their concerns. You may start the conversation by saying something like you would like to simplify their lives through de-cluttering and take on new approaches to owning things. Then you may ask how they feel about living with fewer things. Of course, it may not get the traction that you want at first but a non-threatening approach is the best way you can broach the subject.

When you are listening, repeat their concerns back to them in your own language. Ask if what you are saying is the way they feel. On top of making sure that you comprehend, it will also help them feel that you are on the same page and that you have a great attitude toward the situation, which is not aggressive. You should note this step would best be done in a one-on-one setting. That means family meetings including everyone is a no-no if you want to discuss minimalism for the first time. That is because every individual is going to feel more listened to and valued when it is only the two of you. That is the best way to approach such a sensitive subject. Otherwise, you may risk making the family feel like they are being steamrolled, and forced to take on something which they did not endorse in the first place.

Explain Yourself

Once you have listened and communicated on a one-on-one basis to each of the family members, you should go on to explain the reasons you are drawn to minimalism and the things that you hope to accomplish.

Love and Reassurance

It is crucial to show love to your family and friends and reassure them in the manner that they need so that they become reassured. Even if you think that your family members know why you are adopting minimalism, they still need reassurance that the changes are going to benefit the relationship rather than detract from it. Remember to choose your battles. So, you can tell your spouse clearly before they start to become insecure about things, that you are not phasing them out of your life but you are actually doing it so that you can have more time for them and so that you can be happier as a couple. You should consider the fact that fear from other people that are not as close is a sign that you are growing.

Various Methods to Introduce

There are many reasons behind the approach to minimalism and different attitudes behind doing this. There are some family members who may be motivated by the compassion illustrated by caring for the environment. Others would be motivated more by the aesthetic potential. Others will be inspired by the adventure they can imagine if they travel the world with what could fit into one bag. Others might be frustrated because they are not able to find their favorite things in the clutter and so they will appreciate the minimalist approach. A 17-year-old teen may be ready to save their money for the things that they want such as a camera, car or anything else which is valuable and so you might be able to show them how minimalism can help them achieve that objective.

Younger Children

When it comes to getting children on board with the minimalist approach, you may have to appeal to their sense of what is fun along with personalities. For children of a certain age, just doing things that their parents are doing is all the fun they need in their life because it is both a bonding and educational experience for them. A number of children also have particular fascinations with cleaning devices such as mops and vacuum cleaners so you might tell them that when the floor is clear then they can vacuum. This may only work for a number of months or years but by that time you will have instilled some of the minimalist values you are championing, if nothing else. For example, if your child says that they want a toy, you can say they can have one after they have de-cluttered some of the toys they are no longer using. Give them a chance to choose which ones to discard. This will encourage them not to hoard or hold on to things which are no longer useful to them.

Share Your Reasoning

Share with the family the particular reasons as to why you would like a simple life for you and for them. Tell them about working less so you can do fun things together.

Help them to understand that you want to simplify the home and your life so that you can spend better-quality time with them and have a better attitude toward things. Show them that it will reduce your stress and make you less irritable which is better for everyone around you, especially them. Give them particular examples as well. For example, fewer toys mean less time for the children to arrange their rooms. Fewer things to do for mother and father would also mean more time they get to spend with the children as a family.

Bring on the Compassion

Make your family discuss other people and the reasons they can give to other people. Use the minimalism theme to have your family think about what they can do for the community in terms of charity. This can turn a minimalist exercise into a cause that would benefit those who are less fortunate. Encourage them to think about others and develop positive human aspects like empathy and kindness which is increasingly rare in this society.

Love Over Clean

Your relationships are more important than de-cluttering. If minimalism is the constant cause of strife within your relationships especially with family then you need to take a break. Allow for a difference of opinion. But do not let their clutter make you give up on your journey towards a simpler existence. Minimalist living is going to benefit your life even if you just apply it to the domains within your home and life which you have control over. It is okay to just apply it to your things and leave your family alone if it is not worth the conflict. One has to pick their battles. On the other hand, a clean and clutter-free home is healthier and happier for every member of the house and it is worth the effort required to introduce this lifestyle to every individual within the family.

What Will My Friends Think?

In this scenario, you are paying off debts, de-cluttering, staying off social media and you are eating better. Soon you start to realize that your relationships are the big assets in your life now but the problem is that your friends are not changing at the same rate. The thing is your friends should not have to change because you are being minimalist. If you loved them before then you can still love them the way they are. There may be changes in the way that you interact with them so as to protect your lifestyle but if they really love you then it is likely that they are going to be open-minded about your new path. Share your lifestyle but do not impose it on the ones who you love. Tell them about your plans to consume less and pay off debt. They will learn from your example rather than the things you say.

In your previous life where you would have engaged in mindless consumption and included expensive dinners out, trips with friends and shopping sprees, consider a number of suggestions.

Go Outside.

As opposed to meeting for lunch, a movie or coffee, you can go for a walk, hike or a game of tennis. You may use the experience in order to connect and boost your heart rate at the same time.

Other community events.

You may not have to be Italian to go to the Italian festival. Consider what is going on in your city or town. The chances are there are a number of free classes and other events to take advantage of. You can challenge friends to suggest an activity and then vote on one each month as a group.

Volunteer together.

Sign up as a collective to work at your local soup kitchen or other organization.

Potluck dinners.

Spending hundreds on dinner, wine, and a generous tip was previously fun but now that you know what is important you can host a dinner at your residence. Or you can set up a barbecue in the park. Everyone can bring a dish or beverage and you may spend more time engaging as opposed to getting the attention of the server.

———

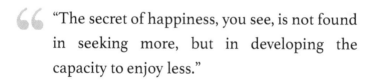 "The secret of happiness, you see, is not found in seeking more, but in developing the capacity to enjoy less."

—*Socrates*

4

TIDY UP

In the United States, minimalism is not exactly a point of pride, so it's especially remarkable that the brutal tidying approach took off in America. This means using a no-nonsense selection and elimination method. By this approach, unless you deeply love an item, then it is not supposed to be within your residence. That would mean the first purging session can indeed be rough even though the euphoria that comes with the unloading of a single bag of unnecessary clutter makes going through the rest of your items that much easier. We've covered the basics of selecting the items you need and the ones that you do not.

When selecting the items to discard, note that the

endgame is not to throw out or donate as much as possible, but to ensure that the things which you are keeping are those which give you the most happiness. This is where you pick up every object that you have and ask if it sparks some form of joy. That may sound like a dull benchmark but if practiced appropriately then it becomes an invaluable tool. It is especially effective when it comes to the organizing of closets as people often develop superficial attachments to clothing and shoes.

Selection

There are minimalists that only have a wardrobe with 10 pieces of clothing, not counting socks and underwear. That may include two jackets, four tops, two pants or one dress and a skirt, one pair of boots and a pair of sneakers or heels/ slippers. This pared down closets give you the basics that can provide different combinations of jeans and tops to alternate during the week and a dress on the weekend. It also allows tops so that you can have one for most days of the week. You can decide to use accessories to mix things up and feel free to adjust this template according to your needs. Make sure that it fits your lifestyle. If you are not the type who wears a blazer, then you may not need one for the closet. Though, if you are the type to wear a jacket every day of the week then maybe two may not be enough. The good news is corporate dress codes are relaxing regardless of whether one works in tech or finance.

Any way that you adjust the list, there are a few characteristics that you want in it. Every piece will need to be as versatile as possible because it must work in different outfit combinations and environments. For example, one may appreciate torn jeans, but you will more likely get better use out of the ones that are dark washed. Neutral color attires like black, gray and white are more easily interchangeable and they can be matched better as compared to the bold patterns which would clash with the ones around you. The other thing is that you ought to choose the items which are high quality. This will increase the lifespan of the attire. You also have to pay a higher premium for those better things as they are going to last longer.

Seasonal

Place a moratorium on purchasing or shopping for attire. For many, shopping for clothes is a time-suck and is always a distraction. In order to start breaking the cycle related to discarding and purchasing, you may have to set a self-imposed buying freeze on everything. The recommended buying freeze duration is 90 days. Given proper time, this exercise in self-discipline is going to change your view of clothing and the stores that sell them. Basically, everything has its own season and you need to set the seasons in which you buy things for yourself and not let yourself be taken in by promotions and advertising. If possible, you can opt to look at every clothing store as an evil enterprise that will stop at nothing to have you buy their products. Have the ultimate negative image concerning the stores but not one against the products. This will make you wary and be better able to rationalize purchase decisions and resist when need be.

Giving Away or Donation

The process of becoming a minimalist for most is not simple in itself. If you have spent the first decades of your life accumulating as many things as possible then getting rid of it is not going to be an overnight process. Unfortunately, the process of reselling things you hope to remove from the house takes an additional amount of concentration. To make things worse, the amount of money that you think you'll earn for each item is usually disappointing. The exceptions would be for those things which are expensive but other than that the effort is not normally worth the financial return.

Excess can become one of the main blessings to other individuals as the items which are in closets, drawers, and basements can still be utilized by another person. If you do not have a need for the item, almost always there will be a person within the immediate community that could use it. There is more evidence than ever that people want to be charitable. If you were in a room full of people and asked them how many wanted to be known for their generous acts, probably all of the hands would go up. There is only a small percentage of individuals that do not want to be generous. This is a thing which most people genuinely want to be true of themselves. The trouble is that for most people they are not able to find the excess so that they can be charitable. Although at the same time their homes are filled with items which they have collected or possessions which have been accumulated and are not in use.

These items can then become the extra which is needed in order to be more generous to the people within the community. As you start to practice minimalism, you begin to find a way to be generous and not just while you are removing possessions, but as your life evolves in the future. Generosity should come as a product of minimalism. Though, generosity is not just the by-product that comes from minimalism as it can also be the motivating factor which helps you to continue on the path towards de-cluttering and minimizing the things you own. If you have recently discovered the happiness of living a more simple life and are starting to be a true minimalist, then you should seriously think about donating the possessions you want to discard. Find a local charity which has ideals that you believe in and donate your things there.

Folding

The way that you fold clothes can be related to the way that someone may load the dishwasher as everyone has their own approach. If you have watched someone load the washer and became horrified at the way they placed the cups and bowls and know that you will have to rearrange everything later on. The same can apply when it comes to folding clothes. There is a brutally strict approach for de-cluttering as it pertains to folding. The objective of these folding techniques is storing the clothes in a vertical manner as opposed to the horizontal way so that you can access the jacket, blazer or jumper more easily than if it were at the bottom of the pile.

The goal is also to fold items and adhere to the method

and then adjust as it concerns the placements of the folds, depending on the mode of the material and the size of that garment. If you keep doing it then you will find the sweet spot. This is the right placement of folds to make sure the garment is flat and taut so that it can stand upright. If done correctly the items including t-shirts are going to stand unaided and individual in a drawer as the patterns or logos will be visible along the top edge so you can easily see what is there. Having selected the one you need, you have the option to pull it out and because the adjacent shirts would support their weight they are not going to collapse. Every item would come with an independent sweet spot which does not have to mean there would be more creases and wrinkles happen when there is pressure exerted on the clothes when they are set in a pile in the drawer with the weight from the items on top pressing on the lower items. When they are stored vertically then there will be no pressure so the wrinkles and creases will not be squashed in.

As you diligently go through your items, folding and then storing, you adjust the level of storage space which is usually the right amount. Follow this approach of keeping only that which brings happiness and speaks to your heart and you will be left with exactly the right amount of things which would fit into your abode. The other thing is all these possessions can be organized in a neat manner and arranged with the use of the storage solutions that are already present.

Shoeboxes are also a number one storage option apparently. They have the perfect height in order to fit into drawers to create dividers. If you would like, once you have finished the ordeal of placing your house in order then you can spend time looking for and getting storage solutions with more appeal, but in the meantime, it would be good to use what is available to finish the task at hand. Also, don't underestimating the noise related to written information that can steal attention of your brain. Remove the labels from boxes or store them so that the information faces the wall as opposed to your field of vision. In this way, if you remove all visual information which does not give happiness, you eliminate the subconscious noise and create an environment which is calmer and more peaceful.

You might also find that shoeboxes are quite useful when it comes to organizing underwear and sock drawers. The lucky thing is that there are online videos which illustrates how to fold and store the garments. The other clothing faux pas which people have been committing this entire time is folding the socks over each other. That seemingly innocuous and sensible action of folding the top of one sock over the other to keep them paired in the drawer has been the wrong approach. Doing this apparently initiates a level of tension within the elastic which means the socks will not properly rest. Socks work very hard every day as they suffer so that the feet can be comfortable. The time when they are in the drawer is when the elastic gets to relax. Through storing them in a non-relaxing state, you do not allow them to unwind as this is their holiday time. Similarly, the usual method of tossing the pants and socks into the drawer supposedly allows for some of the unfortunates to get jostled to the back where they can be easily forgotten.

The answer to this problem clearly seems to be folding in the right manner. Socks like others would have to be folded so they would be able to stand on end. You place one of them neatly on top of the other and then fold them into neat sections. There are less folds needed for the athletic socks while more folds are needed for the ones which are longer. These vertical, neat packages would then be placed into the shoe box. There would be minimal risk that the socks would also get separated which is what happens all the time as they are smartly folded together which means they will not intermingle with others.

If you keep doing this, you will slowly notice that the socks do seem more resilient like this. People never seem to notice how the old approach creates tension in the elastic. The undergarments too would be folded and placed in rows within the shoeboxes. The tights that had been previously bundled into little bags within the new drawers are also going to need a new mode of being stored. They are too flimsy to be stored in a vertical manner and so they are stored and rolled like sushi so they are stored on their ends so that you would be able to see the swirl. When you first do it, it will be quite arduous as you spend time over the bed folding every item sequentially. Everything is categorized and within each group, everything is ordered. Once the work is done, you will immediately feel the benefits. The room will feel less cluttered.

The top of the small wardrobe, for example, will be clear. Previously it may have had a box of hats or other sewing material and related junk which can be repositioned elsewhere or placed in the discard pile. Place these out of sight and on one of the shelves within the now spacious wardrobe. There is something about storing items on top of the wardrobe even if it is the basket that gives the room a sense of clutter. The other immediate improvement that you may note is the back of your door will probably be clearer. There is usually a row of hooks over there which bustles with coats, scarves and bandanas. These would have been depleted and the chosen ones placed inside the wardrobe for selection on the day of wear.

BOOKS

Switching to Kindle

Kindle presents a host of advantages for the user over physical books which encroach and create a need for space along with the inevitable clutter. As such, they are a viable option when it comes to minimalism. For example, a Kindle weighs about 6 ounces and takes about the same amount of space as one book. Though you have the ability to jam as many books as possible in the device, you can take it anywhere. That beats having to take four or five books on a trip especially when you have to make a dash through the airport because you are about to miss a flight. You carry less weight as well which helps with baggage fees.

There is also the factor of convenience if you decide randomly that you would like to read the Icarus Agenda by Robert Ludlum. There is no need for you to go to a bookstore or even wait for shipping from Amazon Prime. So long you have a strong internet connection, it is possible to read any book you want almost immediately. New releases also tend to be cheaper when it comes to e-readers as opposed to traditional book forms considering the e-books do not have what is referred to as physical presence and so they do not cost as much. Kindle also assists those who take public transportation such as trains and buses because it is much easier to read while standing up on the subway as you can hold the book and turn pages with the same hand. This is not the case with paperback books. This can be done while the other hand seeks support from a rail or a pole. In the case of a traditional book, there is always that moment you have to let go of your support so that you can turn the page. It is at this point that most pray the train or bus will not come to a sudden stop and have inertia throw you to the ground, which may be painful and embarrassing.

Books to Keep

This is not a mandate that you have to discard books which you are not reading or which you have already finished, leaving you with only one or two. It is an encouragement to go through every novel and consider whether you really want to keep it around for the next couple of months or years. These can also be categorized according to desire. There are some books that you would probably want to discard at the time and not feel too bad about it. You may want to discard others within a period of a few months because you predict getting bored with them or finishing them and moving on to the next.

Put them all in categories of desirables, negotiated and undesirables. The books that do not serve any purpose because they have already been read should be the first to go. You can donate them to charity or to friends and family. The first option though is usually the easiest to do. For some reason giving books to friends seems like relocating clutter because there is a low chance they will actually get to read them unless they liked the book in the first place. Then there are those books which were given to you or purchased but you have not gotten around to reading for one reason or another. Unless you have a really hectic schedule, set a time within the next few weeks to begin reading them and if this does not seem like an appealing plan then just give them away. Get out of that in-between realm with objects such as these because you will adopt a collector's mentality and end up with clutter.

Here's an even better idea. Get rid of all your books. When the time comes to read your favorite books again, consider buying the e-book version on your Kindle or e-reader. Eventually, you will have all your books back, but in a much more convenient electronic form, as well as a much smaller footprint on your home.

Digital Music and Movies

Music CDs

Music CDs can take up a ton of space especially if your collection is large. The jewel cases are what make up the bulk of the space. Consider trashing the jewel case and just keeping the actual disc. You could store all your music discs on one plastic spindle, like the spindles that come with a purchase of bulk blank CDs. If you are intent on keeping the paper liner-notes that are inserted inside the jewel case, consider removing it and scanning it into your cloud storage, and then throwing the paper copy away. Once all your CDs are on one spindle, you could decorate or paint the protective cover that comes with the spindle and suddenly, the stack of CDs become an art sculpture. You could also mount the discs directly flat on the wall in interesting patterns. Your entire collection would take up zero space and would serve as interesting and colorful wall art. Think of other ways to store your music discs out in plain sight as artwork. This way they add to the room, instead of detracting from it.

Another approach is to sell, donate or give away all your music CDs. Eliminate them completely along with the CD player, and instead opt for cloud music service. For a trivial monthly fee, you can have access to nearly every song imaginable instantly at your fingertips. Consider it renting music, instead of buying it. Google Play, Apple iTunes, Amazon, and other services offer monthly music subscriptions.

Movies and DVDs

You can consider all the same artwork and sculpture ideas for movie discs. Decorate with them, or stack them on a spindle and throw away the bulky plastic cases. Also consider ditching all your movie discs by selling, donating or giving them away. Most movies are watched only once. Rent your movies from digital streaming services. If there is a special movie that you absolutely love and watch all the time, buy it through a digital streaming service. You pay once and have access to the movie forever. Don't buy any more discs. The same advice applies to bulky VCR tapes.

Papers

Ditch Everything

Papers include those things such as tickets, receipts,

coupons and old paperwork. Unless they are needed for tax returns which are very important by the way, the best thing to do would be to chuck everything. The first step would be collecting all of the paper items in bags, drawers and other places within the home or the office and then placing them in a pile. Go through them piece by piece. The objective would be throwing in the recycling bin anything which is not a necessity like scraps, old bills and the receipts which are out of date. For those important papers that are left over, sort them by groups according to themes. These can be related to finances, school, work or even health. These will be the categories used in order to organize and easily file going forward.

The next step would be digitization. Set aside the objects which you consider that you have to have a paper version of. For example, that could be copies of the tax returns of the previous years in case you get audited in the future. Add them to a paper file which is then labeled in the appropriate grouping which you keep stored in a drawer. For each of the others, set up a filing system online which is similar to the paper system that was there previously. This can be done on a number of platforms such as DropBox, Google Drive or Evernote depending on what makes you comfortable. Snap photos of these documents and then save them to the folder for the relevant category.

Then you can throw these paper versions within the recycle bin. These three steps would be enough to manage the paper. You should not have to be overwhelmed by the paperwork. In making a regular habit of running through the steps above, you will be able to cut down on the paperwork clutter.

Kitchen

The act of practicing minimalism within the kitchen area does not require that you sacrifice on your ability when it comes to making tasty meals. Actually, having less congestion in the kitchen is going to make easier to go in there and make something delicious. Minimalism in the kitchen always begins with the removal of utensils and appliances which you do not need and are not using. This means the kitchen can be de-cluttered in a cheap and fast manner with thoughtful consideration.

The following represents a number of kitchen utensils that you do not need if you want to run a no-frills kitchen. It is neither exclusive nor conclusive. This is just a starting point to help you reassess how much is in your kitchen. If you're truthful with yourself and your situation, you might just identify with it.

1. Crockpot.

This is rather bulky and you are most likely just going to use it once every year. The replacement for it varies via dish but usually, large pots in a low-temperature oven would be the better option. If you really need a crock pot, then you can just borrow one from a friend as they will probably not be always using it.

2. Excessive pots and pans.

These can be simplified down to three pots and three pans as you definitely do not need all of them unless you are cooking five-course meals all the time.

3. Extra coffee mugs.

People rarely ever need more than eight unless you host gatherings more than three times a week which is impractical and most people usually do not have families this big.

4. Breadmaker.

These are usually bulky and they tend to eat up the cabinet space. As a replacement, you can try bread recipes which do not need a maker to execute like the 7 ingredients Muesli Bread.

5. Espresso machine.

For one, you likely do not use this as much as you thought you would. The other thing is to get a good espresso, you usually need equipment that is high quality and the time for adjusting your machinery in order to get the perfect shot. This would not be very practical for the average coffee lover. Instead, you can sell the espresso machine and go to Starbucks when you need a very good espresso.

6. Juicer.

These devices are large and tedious to clean. If you must juice, you can still juice without using a machine.

7. Toaster oven.

If you do not regularly use the toaster, then it is just a space-filler. A regular toaster is adequate or just a traditional oven.

8. Fine China/ heirloom dishes.

The emotional attachment for this one tends to be greater as compared to the realization that you do not ever use them. They are usually for nostalgia as gifts for a wedding or a particular person. You need to consider possessing a portion of them and giving the rest to charity or selling them. This one could be a bit hard to let go of, though.

Bathroom

If you are feeling convinced you would like to continue your minimalist foray into the bathroom then that is great. It is a good place to embark your first foray into simple living. There are tips for getting started on creating the minimalist bathroom. The order of business is to get rid of most of the products. It is time to let go of the nine bottles of body lotion and the random makeup kits that you do not use. Having a minimalist bathroom means having one of everything from conditioner to shampoo. This is not a death sentence for those of you already cringing at the prospect. It just means that you will be clearing away the unnecessary clutter within your life.

Next, you need to tone down on the décor. That is to say, no decorative seashells should be allowed. The objective is to create a clean and simple space. The bathroom is typically a smaller room in the home so any extra decorations would make it feel much more cluttered. You can pick one or two decorative things that you adore and which will not crowd the surfaces. Glass jars are also great for neatly holding any of the items which you do not want to be scattered on the sink or even within the medicine cabinet. Take note that the bathroom needs to be free of clutter even in the places that might not be necessarily visible.

As such, you need to keep most if not all of the surfaces clear. Making the effort to do this thing makes all the difference in the world. Whatever you need to do to make sure that the surfaces stay free of clutter is critical. This is particularly significant for all minimal bathrooms. You need to resist the urge to throw the towels or the clothes on the floor. Cleanliness is very important. Apart from not discarding things everywhere, you need to take time out of your day so that you carefully wipe down surfaces and the toilet. This will provide the bathroom that extra fresh feeling. If you have the ability to do so, you can decide to paint the walls with a creamy ivory color and then throw up a white or sheer curtain.

Advantages of a Minimalist Bathroom

You get to feel more organized. The power of the organization should not be undervalued. In a chaotic system, it is nice for one to have private corners to yourself so that you stay organized regardless of anything else. You should consider how good it is going to feel to walk into a clean bathroom every morning. It will instill more confidence in your step as you start your day.

No Last Minute Cleaning

You will probably not have to go into a deep cleaning frenzy each time that you have guests. When there are fewer things to clean then it will be easier to tidy things before people start to come over. At the same time, in a small environment, there is always a bigger incentive for keeping things clean in any case.

Enlightenment Towards Minimalism

You will probably always feel inspired towards decluttering the rest of your home when the bathroom looks simple and clean. By starting small with the bathroom and other areas, you may begin to understand the true way that minimalism functions. Because it is a very small area of the home, the bathroom is a great place for the experimentation of simple living.

Minimalism with Your Car

The western culture has an affinity for cars as they are a symbol of freedom, affluence and a carefree lifestyle. Consumerism has also created the idea that everyone needs one. Though rather than giving people freedom, cars just saddle you with debt and they affect your health because they limit the level of exercise. The following are some things you can attempt in your journey to go 'car-lite'.

Starting Small

Selling the car can be part of your downsizing process as it is a good financial and health-related decision that you can make. It is definitely going to help you to reduce some of the debt burdens involved with having a car including maintenance, insurance, fuel, and repairs. On the other hand, you can retain one vehicle if you have two, or minimize the use of your single vehicle by leaving it at a garage for a period of time such as a week while you do your errands on foot or by public transportation.

Cost-Benefit Analysis

Even in the event that you have paid off the vehicle, you still need to consider some of the hidden costs. For example, people tend to spend at least a fifth of their income on vehicles. A study that was done by the American Automobile Association also claims that the average citizen spends about $8,410 a year so they can own a car. That equates to an estimated $700 every month. That figure includes the fuel, insurance, parking fees, repairs, washes and oil changes. Taking this into account that would mean owning a car is the second largest household cost in the United States. People may spend more on the vehicle than on food and health. If this is your situation, then the car is detracting from your path in minimalism and you are going to have to make cutbacks in order to free yourself from the financial stresses entailed.

Going Car Lite with the Children

Doing car minimalism with the children can be a hassle but you should not let this be a barrier. There are a number of people that operate car-free and they have children yet they still claim there are benefits to be had by this option. In this case, you will not have to spend thousands of dollars to get a bike so you can get around safely. There is also an abundance of family cargo bikes and trailer options that you can use. You should also not forget to consult with your friends, elders and others that went car-lite and ask questions about the challenges and successes.

Going Multi-Modal

Biking is not the only way that one can get around without the use of a car. You need to consider the use of a bus or train or even walking to your destination. By taking this multi-modal type of approach when it comes to transportation, it will make your life that much more flexible. For example, on the days when it is raining or snowing, you can opt to take the bus or the subway depending on which is more convenient.

———

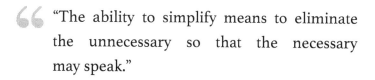 "The ability to simplify means to eliminate the unnecessary so that the necessary may speak."

—*Hans Hofmann*

5

STORAGE

Through being clever about the way you organize your living area and how you employ a few storage techniques, there will not be a need to go to extremes and get rid of every worldly possession. The home can continue to feel as streamlined as it did when you first moved in. The window seats are some of the multi-purpose storage dreams. A source of clutter could be the DVDs and CDs. The solution for this would be the window seating. They are not only one of the best spaces for curling up with some tea and a good book, but they also hide all of the DVDs and CDs which accumulate over the course of time. The best thing about these is they can start to become an after-thought, and they do not always need to be sorted.

On the other hand, you may want the flexibility that comes with storage but do not require a permanent fixture there all of the time. You should consider some mobile storage box options which you can pair with a comfortable cushion on top of the window seating. These would be adequate for the times when you need additional seating for a party or get-together. The other clutter problems would be paper and post. If you have the luck and have a second-floor or split-level within the residence then this may be your untapped storage. One method of using this prime space would be to close it with drawers so that it becomes part of the overall mass of the stair. In the event the stair is near the entry, that would be a good place for things such as bags, shoes, and keys which you would take off when entering and exiting the residence.

Toys may also be a hassle when it comes to storage as they are purchased frequently depending on the number of children, and kids do not always tidy up. The solution, in this case, would be under-floor storage. When you think about caravans and mobile homes, there are a number of storage solutions within the floor and the furniture where you would be able to hide excess clutter. The normal home should not be any different. In this scenario, the floor would be raised and access to the storage space would be via removable panels that are on the floor. There would be no need to sweep the toys under the rug when it is possible to sweep them into the floor. If this is something which you are considering in your home then you ought to be sure that there is sufficient height in your room, as you might end up with a ceiling that is closer than you think. Similarly, toy boxes would be a great idea as they typically lend themselves to being handy by adding a simple top. It could be that you would like to have some fun with your children. As such, you might try finding boxes which are strong and have an afternoon when you may decorate them together.

Minimalist Approaches to Storage

Marie Kondo debuted the Konkari approach in 2011 after she wrote the novel 'The Life-Changing Magic of Tidying up Has Done It Again.' After selling more than four million copies of her book worldwide, she unleashed the storage option which is a set of three empty shoebox style containers in order to assist individuals to organize their living areas. Known as the Hikidashi Boxes which is detailed after the Japanese word for 'drawer', the collection was designed in collaboration with Cecylia Ferrandon, Apple's head of packaging materials. The collection consists of harmony, balance, wonder, and clarity.

Though the venture championed by Kondo is a bit new, it considers the need for small parts and storage systems which play a significant role when it comes to upgrading the living space. In any case, minimalism concerns stripping away the unneeded elements. This is all about focusing on the things that need to be there. One of the ways to do this is incorporating storage systems which are well thought out, and assist the homeowners in reducing the clutter and initiating a clean and streamlined look that is appealing to the eye and adds something timeless and aesthetic along the way. In any case, minimalism does not ever go out of style as a look and will be relevant in home interiors for years to come. The storage solution offered by Kondo is not the only choice when one is looking to add beauty to the residence using this type of system. A number of other brands provide storage units which allow for both function and aesthetic within the minimalist residence.

Lundia storage units are a storage system which minimalists can opt for by the Lundia furniture company which deals in storage solutions. The compartments allow for three different sizes as inspired by the ISO 2016 paper system. This was designed by Joanna Laajisto and entails handmade boxes that are smaller than A3, A4, and A5 in size. They are also made from glue laminated solid pine which is joined with wooden pin connections. That particular sizing system allows for the boxes to stack on top of each other using different configurations.

Smaller storage systems may not be very familiar, but homeowners can utilize stacked storage systems or units for shelves like the stacked configurator by Muuto. Through the use of small clips, the modules are rearranged so they would allow for diversified varieties of shelving setups, side tables or room dividers. The stacked configurator from Muuto as an art piece allows for a sufficient amount of storage space and adds a particular edge to the apartment.

———

 "Focus and simplicity. Simple can be harder than complex: You have to work hard to get your thinking clean to make it simple. But it's worth it in the end because once you get there, you can move mountains."

—*Steve Jobs*

6

PETS

We adore our pets. They're fuzzy, cuddly, and loyal. We cherish them and love them, and the connection between us increases every day. But with owning pets comes "stuff." Dog beds, grooming supplies, toys, medicine, collars, clothing, blankets, and more. We spoil our pets year after year convinced their life is somehow better with all the things we provide. When you think about it, it's obvious to see that the amount of "things" we purchase for them is more for us and our satisfaction. We buy the overindulgent treats, we splurge on the special toy, and we dress our pets in expensive clothing. Why?

You may imagine a life of minimalism is not plausible with pets, but it's actually amazingly simple. There's one thing you must know: Pets don't need a lot. The quickest way to make your pet happy is to love it. If you ask your veterinarian what a pet needs to thrive and have a beneficial experience, you'll likely hear some of these: food, medicine, shelter, water, proper grooming, flea and tick protection, and exercise.

Easy, right? Your home and a water bowl already cover water and shelter. A few grooming items, like a brush and shampoo, will occupy a single drawer. The flea and tick protection and other medicine can be acquired as needed, saving space. If you decide to buy in bulk, they don't take up much space and can comfortably fit in the same drawer with your grooming stuff. Playing fetch or tug-of-war outside leaves you with only a few toys. If there is one toy, in particular, your pet loves, then keep it. And finally, food. A small case can fit into a kitchen cabinet or pantry. A large bag might need a more significant place. Combined with a bowl, you've now taken up a small corner in your home. The total space for everything mentioned is a drawer and a small patch of floor.

Consider using furniture in a new way to provide for your pet. Engineer the bottom drawer of a piece of furniture to house your food and water bowls. Just pull out the drawer and instantly, you are feeding the little fur ball. When your pet is finished eating, just close the drawer, and once again the area looks clean and tidy.

However, you may find the occasional item that both you and your pet cherish such as a scratching post or comfy bed. Before splurging, be sure to think about for whom you're really buying the item. Will it bring pleasure to your furry loved one, or are you buying it because it is "adorable"?

During your experience with minimalism, you should also minimize the things for your pets. Donate items that seldom get used to pet shelters. Recycle items that are worn out or can't be restored. For the other things, like clothing, determine whether they serve a purpose or if they are just for you. Once you're done, you can breathe easy at all the extra floor space. With lots of love, your furry friend will undoubtedly be a happy one.

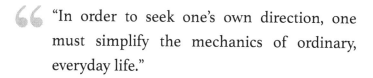 "In order to seek one's own direction, one must simplify the mechanics of ordinary, everyday life."

—*Plato*

7

50 QUICK TIPS TO HELP YOU GO MINIMAL

I have included a list of 50 quick things you can easily do right now to get started on your journey toward minimalism. Not all these things will be right for you, but they are good suggestions none the less. Some of these are geared toward frugality, which is just another form of minimalism where finances are the focus.

1. Make an inventory for everything.

You may not be able to decide what to cut, up to the point that you have a list of everything that you have in your possession. That may take some time and the time it takes to catalog the materials may prove that you have too many things. When you have knowledge of what you have, categorize it, and this can be done sequentially from room to room by the frequency of use or by the purpose.

2. Live in a smaller house.

Just because you are able to afford a big house, it should not be cause for you to go all out and buy a big one. You can opt for a small house and still be comfortable. This is not to recommend you should opt for a one-room rental in the inner city. You can save huge sums of money per year by living in a smaller house, and this will be useful when you least expect it.

3. Go to events with one vehicle.

You can also be able to save on fuel and other hassles by going to places or road-trips with one car. For one, you will lessen the liability of breakdowns and accidents by half. Though there will be less space in the vehicle, there will be overall better security if you use one vehicle for travel. In the family situation, it will decrease the costs of fuel, servicing, and repairs.

4. Rent rather than own.

This one is quite controversial as people have different ideas on it. You should not always just assume that purchasing would be the better option. In the event that you calculate the interest as you pay the mortgage, insurance, and maintenance then you might find that buying is going to be more costly as compared to renting. If you rent and save that money, then you can invest the difference and actually end up in a better position within a few years. This is not a given. In every situation, you can lose the investment. It depends on your preferences and situation.

5. Look for used first.

It may sound like being cheap but there are a lot of things that you can get which are second hand but they are high quality or a lightly used and so as are good as new. You should see if anyone that you know has one which they are not using or do not need anymore. You may also send out a text or email to friends and family or even just ask around. You may be surprised. For example, you may be about to buy something then you discover that your father or mother just bought the same thing and have no need for the previous version of what they bought, say a phone, car or table.

If no one that you know owns that which you want to buy, you can get great deals on e-bay or craigslist provided you do your due diligence. You may also opt to look for the item at sales or even thrift shops. You may find a good bargain if you look around.

6. Do not be too Spartan.

This may seem like the opposite to what minimalism is preaching even though 100 item minimalism standards are not about denying yourself all facets of pleasure. On the contrary, it is about finding it in simplicity. In this case, you ought to end up with items which are going to make you happy and make things easier for you in the end. Scaling back does not necessarily mean that you deny yourself life's pleasures. There's a difference between frugality and being minimalistic.

7. Re-purge.

Three months after selling or donating those possessions which you do not want or are not using, you need to reassess all of the remaining possessions and then redo the purge exercise to get rid of those things which you are not using at least once a month. That is the thing about the minimalist lifestyle. It is a lifestyle and not a one-time thing which means you must keep trying to aspire to maintain a constant level of simplicity in your life instead of just doing a mass purge and leaving it at that. Do not be afraid of ditching something which might come in handy in the future. There are chances that you have a good neighbor that is going to lend you that crockpot when you need to cook for extra guests.

8. Use the 12-month rule.

Discard everything which you have not used in the previous year. That includes the Christmas decorations old shirts and skirts, jeans and utensils. Even that sewing machine that you were given to fix but have not yet touched needs to go. If you have not touched within the course of a year, the chances are that you are probably not going to use or fix it in the near future so just admit it to yourself.

9. Eat out less.

This one is self-explanatory if you are a fan of going to eat then you need to rein that in for the sake of financial relief and waste because you can probably satisfy yourself with a home-cooked meal.

10. Commute by bicycle.

Even if you own a car, you may want to try this option as it can go a long way health-wise and save on transportation fees and time as bikes are not caught in traffic the way cars are.

11. Walk.

Often times you may find yourself driving to the corner store even if it is a distance which you can easily walk, or to a school that is less than two miles away. Instead, you can walk and burn off some of the latent calories and do yourself a favor.

12. Sell your clutter.

This is more about making money than saving on finances. As such, you can hold a garage sale and sell them for a discount or do it on e-bay depending on where the market would be more attracted to it.

13. Take care of business.

In the event that you own a home office, you may think there are things you cannot live without such as fax machines, printers or desks. Your needs will vary as depending on which field you are in though there are services like EchoSign which are making printing out contracts a thing of the past.

This way, you have the ability to send your faxes for free from FaxZero, and you may even use a laptop with a cooling lap as opposed to sitting on a desk the whole day.

14. Own a minimalist wardrobe.

It's not for everyone but here is a good tip or the minimalist lifestyle. You should aim to own neutral colors in your clothing such as black, white or gray as they are easily interchangeable even if you have a small amount of clothing in your lineup. That then saves the stress of picking outfits, and you won't need as many clothes.

15. Resist impulse buying.

It does not matter what it is, every time you make a purchase you are now accountable to a checklist of the reasons you are getting it. Not all of them will pass the test and on these ones just let them go and get the items that really matter to you.

16. Do not go on a food shopping spree when you are hungry.

You may have heard this before but when you buy a lot of food thinking that you will eat it all simply because you are hungry, go with the inner voice that tells you, you are overreacting. This also applies when you are eating out especially. Sometimes, our stomachs are being too greedy for our own good.

17. Use a 30-day list In order to curb impulse buying.

You may create a 30-day list. If you want to buy something that is not a necessity, then you can opt to place it on that list and add a date to that designation. Make it a rule that you cannot buy the thing for less than 30 days after placing the item on the list. That will give you time so that you can deliberate on how much you want it. After a month, if you still want it, then you can go ahead and buy the item.

18. Only keep the multipurpose objects.

Try not to keep those objects which do not serve multiple objectives within the house. If it only does one particular thing, then you may need to put in in the discard pile so that you can make room for something which has more than one particular use. For example, a couch which can double up as a bed is perfect when guests visit you. It could also be a coffee table which also serves as a work desk.

19. Use the library.

As opposed to buying books on Amazon, you can make the option to visit the local library when you have time and read that book which you have been looking for. The average person allegedly spends almost $2,000 every year on entertainment alone which is not inclusive of eating out, so there is a percentage of that which goes to books. This is not to say that you should go without, but there are better and more frugal ways to entertain yourself.

20. Frugal exercise.

Instead of using your money on gym memberships at exclusive clubs you can opt for exercise at home. You can buy some of the equipment and follow regimens which are posted online most of the time unless of course, you are training professionally then you are going to need expert advice. However, if you are doing it for your own fitness goals, then the same can be accomplished at home with the right diet, discipline and exercise schedule.

21. Use carpool or public transportation.

With the use of the bus or walking, there are several ways to get around the transportation cost associated with a personal vehicle. You can seek the help of a neighbor and pay them a fee especially if your work is in the same direction.

On the other hand, there is public transportation. Taxi, bus, and train are all there depending on which is preferable considering where you live.

22. Try to stay healthy.

This sounds like an oxymoron because no one knows when they are going to get sick but you can be proactive by exercising, eating right or just self-preservation. Staying healthy is going to save a ton of doctor's bills on checkup, surgeries, and medication.

23. Frugal approaches to gifting.

Gifts cost a lot of money over the year especially if you have a lot of friends and each of them expects a present on their birthday and during the holidays. As such you can opt to make your gifts as opposed to buying every few months or so. They will also appreciate the fact that you took the time to make them.

24. Reduce alcohol intake.

Buying and consuming alcohol on a regular basis among other things reduces inhibitions that you may have which leads you to make purchases and bad decisions. You may want to limit your consumption so that you do not end up complicating your life more than you need to, in order to continue on the path toward minimalism.

25. Quit smoking.

This is an addiction so it may not be the easiest thing to do but it is definitely a health basic if you want to steer clear of complications during your later years. You will save money otherwise spent on the cigarettes, not to mention the long-term medical costs involved.

26. Drink water.

Usually, people are not aware of the health risks posed by

the alcohol and soft drinks they consume, which have a lot of calories and incur costs in terms of health considerations. If you have an indulgent lifestyle, you need to drink a lot of water as a precaution to flush toxins out of your body, which saves on health issues you may have in the future.

27. Batch the errands.

As opposed to doing things individually such as going somewhere on Monday and then going somewhere else on Tuesday, you can save on time and fuel by going to both or three places in one day and getting it over with. That way you can free up an entire day with which to do what you want and relax. Also, you can opt to pay as much of the bills online as possible so that you eliminate some of the errands during the process.

28. Stop the use of your credit cards.

You may use just one especially if you do not like carrying cash but only when you have to because they represent triggers for debt. They offer a false sense of security for buying things that you are convinced you have a need for. They make the act of buying things all too easy and so you end up spending money you don't have, resulting in immense debt. Apparently, the average American with 1 credit card is in about $8,500 of debt which is no small figure.

29. Cancel email subscriptions.

This has been previously mentioned because emails from different platforms are auto-generated to give you information which you probably do not need concerning causes or events that you no longer support. The only way to get rid of overwhelming emails is to cancel the subscription through the link near the bottom of the email titled "unsubscribe."

30. Stay at home.

This is self-explanatory and cures a lot of problems which can disrupt your minimalist lifestyle. Part of being a minimalist is minimizing the liabilities in one's life including basic exposure to risk. Anytime you walk out the door, you are exposed to all sorts of risks, and this is not within the plan of minimalism.

31. Do things yourself.

As opposed to hiring someone to do something, you can opt to do it yourself. It may take a lot of time and effort, but with the assistance of YouTube videos and good motivation, you can have things in hand. This is regardless of whether you are working on a table from Ikea or your car. There is also a certain satisfaction that being able to fix things by yourself brings that is not replicable.

32. Make your own things.

This could take a bit more time and effort, but it may be a bit of fun. Especially if it is a family project, then it is something that you can do together as a bonding experience to enhance the level of your relationships with each other.

33. Avoid convenience foods.

Also known as fast food, you may want to avoid these as they increase health risks and they add an element of waste to your lifestyle which is completely contradictory to the minimalist lifestyle that is encouraged.

34. Travel using frugal means.

It is not worth it to travel everywhere by air if there are other means available for you. You can opt for the train or the bus if they have the same destination stops because they are much cheaper. You end up saving more money and possibly get richer experiences when you carpool or go for a road trip to the same place. If you must fly and you are flexible on your travel dates, consider using a website like skyscanner.com to find the cheapest month and day to travel.

35. Stop paying interest.

Any type of loan be it a mortgage, auto loan or personal loan incurs interest which is not minimalistic. Only have the most significant loans but do not take on any more if it is possible because these tend to complicate one's life and place a strain on the finances.

36. Cut your own hair.

While on the subject of things you can do on your own, hair can be managed without having to go to a salon unless you are a media personality or model. It can be managed by friends and family according to your preferences or even by yourself. This tends to work better for men, but it's also possible for women.

37. Cut cell phone use.

Smartphone addiction is a means of filling your time, which is not healthy for your relationships in the long run. You develop a bigger attachment to social media than to your children, and this is against the minimalistic handbook which advocates cutting off ties with the harmful distractions of the outside world.

38. Avoid holiday promotions.

The holidays are the prime time corporations maximize purchases from people, and so they offer most of their promotions at this time because people are in the mood. If you are not careful, you may find yourself spending and buying more than you bargained. Plan a budget for all holidays and stick by it.

39. Maintain things.

The reason we sometimes buy things is that the old stuff wears out. Sometimes when money is not an issue we are not careful with things and end up buying things over and over which is a waste and in contradiction with minimalism because we end up with a lot of clutter of the old broken down versions.

40. Cut down on social media.

This is part of the theme to cut down on one's online presence because it can become a time filler and addiction which detracts from personal relationships and experiences.

41. Buy clothes on sale.

Instead of buying new clothes from expensive stores, you can get good clothes from the thrift shop and at a bargain and enjoy them for years. You will save a ton of money which can be channeled to other things.

42. Plan ahead.

This is easy to say, but it is hard to implement. Though if you make it a habit of thinking ahead to matters in your life, then you can save a lot of revenue.

43. Telecommute.

This does not necessarily give you a dream life, but it allows you to save on transport and dictate your hours in a way. You also have the chance to control your home environment which people who work 9 to 5 cannot do as easily.

44. Sun-dry your clothes.

This may sound Amish, but it does save on power and having a dryer which is also cumbersome and costly. The other benefit is your clothes will last longer.

45. Eat less sugar and starch.

This is purely for health purposes as this is usually the main source of poor health. It will also save you the cost and suffering from arthritis, obesity, diabetes, and heart disease in the future.

46. Cook in advance.

This is to save you from the laziness which may occur when you wait to have supper at night and end up ordering out. You may also opt to cook in advance for the whole week to save time so that you retrieve it from the fridge when you need it.

47. Wash your clothes less.

Some people wear clothes and wash them the next day. You may opt to wear them again if they are not dirty. Most of the time, you may find they are still presentable, and this saves on washing.

48. Save on gas.

Considering the state of the economy and the price of gas you may opt to use the car less or use it for multiple errands at the same time.

49. Eat economical meals.

Save money by going for combinations which are economical depending on your periodic budget.

50. Save on the groceries.

Buy things in bulk from wholesale rather than retail stores and store them so that you do not have to keep going for shopping. It may also be because you do not want to spend too much money and you have a large family to feed.

———

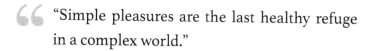 "Simple pleasures are the last healthy refuge in a complex world."

—*Oscar Wilde*

8

BENEFITS OF MINIMALISM

When you clear out unnecessary activities and items from your life, there are unexpected results. There is a sense of purpose which comes. You tend to feel motivated to do what you have set out to accomplish, and you have more energy to implement it because your vision is clear and you do not have any confusion.

Self Confidence

Previously you may have thought that the right things like clothes and cars would have helped you get the right amount of confidence to achieve your goals. When you practice minimalism in the right way you start to feel good about yourself without the material gifts as a crutch, and that is quite powerful as it makes you quite formidable.

This is one of the unexpected benefits that come with living with less.

More Time

When you get rid of the excess things and limit wasteful experiences, you may be worried that you will get bored, but you will slowly start to adapt to the new structure of your life which is refreshingly healthy. As a result, you find yourself unusually happier or in better moods most of the time and able to be there for your spouse and children when they need you because you have more time to yourself.

Less Stress

Imagine living in a universe where you don't come home to a cluttered house, or you did not have to wake up early on a Saturday morning to do something you did not want to do in the first place. You will have fewer conflicts, and so you are more at peace and have an overall happier existence as compared to people that have different commitments and hang-ups that they are not able to get over.

Better Health

By reducing your intake of alcohol, stopping smoking,

and reducing the times that you eat out you may effectively be cutting your health risks in half and giving your body the chance to replenish its reserves allowing for better health and energy. Minimalism will enable you to scale back on those things which cause you mental, emotional and physical stress so that you are able to have an optimal life and have better relationships with your loved ones.

Extra Money

This should come as no surprise. When you adopt minimalism, you are saying no to excessive eating out, no to ordering things online and no to shopping, all of which puts a dent in your finances. It should be logical then that you are probably going to have more money at the end of the month if you do none of these things. You also get to explore your philanthropic side because you will be donating some of your things to the poor or to a cause which you believe in.

You Provide a Good Example to Your Children

When you adopt minimalism, de-cluttering is one of the first themes which mean cleaning out the house and keeping it that way. This provides a good example to the children who will then adopt it for cleaning their rooms and play areas. They will grow up to be tidy and self-sufficient, which is a great gift in this current age. You will also instill the values of charity and kindness when you give the unwanted things to the poor. As such, it is going to teach them to get rid of things which do not provide any value to them, which is not taught a lot of time.

Visual Appeal

When you de-clutter the house and go from the living room to the kitchen, bathroom, and bedroom, you make it visually appealing. You do not have to clean it regularly. When visitors come, you create a good impression that you have things in order because you have tidied up so much. It makes the rooms appear neat and organized in a way that was not possible before. The car and garage areas are also almost always presentable, and you get to store a large number of things in a small area with the use of the Kondo approach.

———

 "Simplicity is making the journey of this life with just baggage enough."

—*Charles Dudley Warner*

9

SUCCESS STORIES

Minimalism is essentially a more conservative and humane way to approach life. Most people would honestly prefer owning things, including me, but there is a saying that all we own is vanity and we carry nothing with us to the grave. However, the reason most people work is to earn so they can possess things and lead better lives. Take a random group of people and ask them why they are working and I can guarantee you a large percentage of those people will tell you their main motivation is money and things. Although there is something peculiar I noticed; those who got to the highest levels of their potential all had one story, they were driven by a purpose larger than money. A minimalist, in essence, does away with anything that will push one away from their purpose or what they are interested in, meaning that for the minimalists, money is a bonus.

It is a common theory and way of doing things that have been deployed over and over again through the years and below are some success stories by the most influential of people aging back years and how they led minimalist lives and how it was reflected in the daily lives and routines.

The first person we look at was once the world's richest man. Apple's very own founder Steve Jobs, he was a believer of the concept, and this was reflected with what he stood for even at work. He had his slogan of simplifying complexity and portrays it in all his designs since then. He shared this agenda and even taught it in business, that it's not the sophistication of the product you offer, but how you approach the customer with its simplicity. This did not apply just to his work though, it is also a way of living he believed in and followed in his home; he had almost no furniture and had a portrait of Einstein who he looked up to, a Tiffany lamp, one chair and finally one bed. He didn't believe in having more than necessary and was extremely careful with what he had.

The other individual we look at is the man Steve looked up to, Einstein, the most renowned scientist of all time. He was also a firm believer of this concept of minimalism and hence the impact it left on some of his followers including Steve Jobs. Just like Steve, Einstein was rich. The only difference is that he gave away a large portion of his income to the less fortunate and owned very few pieces of clothing for himself. Just like his follower and admirer Steve, Einstein had his taste for things he spent his money on including expensive cigars, coffee, and some musical instruments. This was his go-to when it came to earthly pleasures.

The other success story on a minimalist we can look at is a famous Canadian artist who also lived a minimalist life and believed in living free. Jane Siberry was a minimalist who lived a minimalist life and justified this by always having not more than two bags on her tours, her guitar, and her laptop as she traveled from one region to the other sharing her music. Other than her possessions, as an artist, her only way to get income from music was to sell her music albums as most artists do. She did not that and instead had all her tracks available for streaming and download for free on her website. She eventually got tired of being pressured by executives from major recording labels and quit, selling most of her belongings and remaining in a single home. She prefers to spend her time now roaming most of the world exploring.

There is something that stands out about these three

people even before moving to the other examples of minimalistic success stories. All of them served a purpose greater than themselves and believed in bettering the lives of the less fortunate and raising the standard in their field. There is a point to be drawn from that; if you were to get into this for financial reasons, you might end up failing in whatever it is you were driven to attain.

The next individual we will look at who lives a minimalistic life is Leonardo Da Vinci. To him, simplicity is the ultimate sophistication. He spent his revenue feeding his friends. Rich or poor, he believed that their wellbeing was his wellbeing and that was a factor they appreciated a lot.

Socrates, who is a very important man to the western world believed that as human beings we should be more concerned with seeking virtue which would make our lives better than to seek material wealth that would divide us and cause war. He stated that to him the key to happiness or the secret to happiness is not found in looking for more, but in the ability to be happy with less.

Minimalists do not value materialistic possessions as seen from the individuals above, but it does not hinder their success stories. These are the most known and respected people in their fields, but because of their minimalistic nature and ability to serve a purpose beyond themselves they stood out from the rest and remain today as symbols of charity and giving. Minimalists don't necessarily deny themselves of everything, as we have seen, and they all have their guilty pleasures. To them, it's about having enough, not a lot.

———

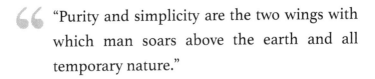

"Purity and simplicity are the two wings with which man soars above the earth and all temporary nature."

—*Thomas Kempis*

CONCLUSION

Minimalism is not about self-deprivation. Rather, it is about your mental, physical, emotional and financial health. It is about analyzing and knowing yourself, what works for you, and what does not. You need to take time and evaluate what is really important in your life and whether or not lack of it would hinder you from living the life you want. If it doesn't, then you probably don't need it.

Minimalism also is not just about materialistic things, it is also about emotional and psychological growth. For you to move forward, there are things you need to do, and it might involve dropping some of the company you keep. You need to be mindful of the people you surround yourself with as they directly impact who you end up becoming.

Other than people, you also need to understand that minimalism can be deployed in your health. Choosing to eat healthier, burn calories by taking the stairs, or cycling to work are examples of minimalistic choices you can make as an individual. They are going to benefit you as an individual and better your life quality as a whole. The other aspect of life to which you can apply minimalism is key; your finances. I look at many people especially in developing nations, and they all take pride in the ownership of material possessions, especially cars. What they don't understand is that a car can be a liability or it can be an asset depending on the individuals who purchase it.

The problem is not about you purchasing the car you prefer. It boils down to the fact that in some countries you find a family of say three people who own four or five vehicles, and three are used every morning with individuals who are going the same route. If you sit down and put this into perspective, and consider the amount of fuel consumption, you will be shocked. These amounts could have been put to better use, or even the sale of the extra cars would have allowed for a better car that would have served them for longer and saved them money.

Minimalism as a thought and way of life should be encouraged in society. The reason being, most of the chaos and issues that are faced in the world are as a result of people being materialistic, and that drives them to take any course of action to amass wealth. Corruption cases are always about an individual who tries to benefit himself and his circle at the expense of the rest. Understanding the concept of minimalism and putting it all into perspective would allow us to appreciate and enjoy what we have and would calm the urge to have more.

Spiritually and mentally you can also improve your life by being a minimalist. In this perspective, we mean being able and ready to let go, knowing when it is time to let go and when as a minimalist it is better to let go. It puts clarity and perspective into your life as it allows you to focus on what and who matters most in your life. In putting energy into what matters, you reap rewards that you actually want and appreciate, hence bettering your life.

Minimalism is to an extent an art that you learn the older you get. Having the ability to know what you really need in your life and removing everything you do not gives you so much time and shows you whether you are making any progress in life. It also reveals when old problems are still reoccurring and preventing you from achieving your potential or serving your purpose in life. Especially in this modern era where the virtual world gives people a sense of false hope. Being a minimalist helps you get some perspective and much-needed clarity to guide you and put you a step above as seen in our case studies.

Joel Osteen said that he wished everyone could get what they wish for, and buy and do everything they ever wanted to do and then, just then would we all realize that it is not all that. There is more to life. Fulfillment does not come from materialistic possessions instead it comes from the meaningful memories we share as a people with the ones we love and respect. That serving humanity gives the deepest sense of fulfillment. Minimalists understand this and hence dedicate their lives to a greater purpose than just the average human being and so lead happy, fulfilled and quality lives.

Set time aside to analyze your habits. Do you need all the food you eat? Do you need seventy pairs of shoes and four closets of clothes, or do you need six cars to get you through your day? Take time to analyze your life seriously and remove all that you don't need. Choose to use those resources or that energy you spent on a negative friend or a stressful girlfriend on something that is going to build you as an individual and help you grow. That is the greatest fulfillment there is.

There isn't a life that's better than yours. If we all find our purpose and get satisfied with what is ours, and accept it, and use what we have, we end up having a greater meaning of life. Much of what bothered us and lowered our quality of life disappears. Some of the people we reviewed in our case study led the happiest lives we have seen and long ones at that because they saw something the common mind could not.

" Minimalism is beautiful and should be embraced.

—*Kiku Katana*